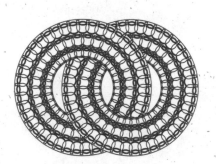

WHEN DID WE
STOP BEING CUTE?

WHEN DID WE STOP BEING CUTE?

MARTIN WILEY

CavanKerry Press

PRESS

CavanKerry Press Ltd.
Fort Lee, New Jersey
www.cavankerrypress.org

Publisher's Cataloging-in-Publication Data
provided by Five Rainbows Cataloging Services
Names: Wiley, Martin, author. | Amador, Nico, writer of foreword.
Title: When did we stop being cute? / Martin Wiley ; foreword by
    Nico Amador.
Description: Fort Lee, NJ : CavanKerry Press, 2023.
Identifiers: ISBN 978-1-933880-97-6 (paperback)
Subjects: LCSH: Novels in verse. | Racism—Fiction. | Popular music—
    Fiction. | New Jersey—Fiction. | Bildungsromans. | Poetry,
    Modern—21st century. | BISAC: POETRY / American / African
    American & Black. | POETRY / Subjects & Themes / Family. |
    FICTION / Coming of Age.
Classification: LCC PS3623.I44 W54 2023 (print) | LCC PS3623.I44
    (ebook) | DDC 811/.6—dc23.

Cover photograph: Rachel Bellinsky/Stocksy United
Cover and interior text design by Ryan Scheife, Mayfly Design
First Edition 2023, Printed in the United States of America

CAVANKERRY
PRESS

Made possible by funds from the
New Jersey State Council on the Arts, a partner
agency of the National Endowment for the Arts.

CavanKerry Press is grateful for the support it receives from the
New Jersey State Council on the Arts.

In addition, CavanKerry Press gratefully acknowledges generous
emergency support received during the COVID-19 pandemic from the
following funders:

The Academy of American Poets

Community of Literary Magazines and Presses

The Mellon Foundation

National Book Foundation

New Jersey Arts and Culture Recovery Fund

New Jersey Council for the Humanities

New Jersey Economic Development Authority

Northern New Jersey Community Foundation

The Poetry Foundation

US Small Business Administration

Also by Martin Wiley

Just/More (2021)

. . . the youth
are getting restless, yeah

—Bad Brains,
"The Youth Are Getting Restless"

CONTENTS

PART TWO: HEY KID WALK STRAIGHT, MASTER YOUR HIGH

PART THREE: BUT LIFE IS JUST A PARTY & PARTIES WEREN'T MEANT TO LAST

EPILOGUE: I THOUGHT WE'D GET TO SEE FOREVER . . .

FOREWORD

At 4, we were precious,
I said to Pete & Danny.
By 8, precocious.

& 10,

dangcrous.

—Martin Wiley

As someone who wasn't born a boy but later became one, I have often tried to picture what my teens and early twenties would have been like if I hadn't had to negotiate the particular challenge of being trans. Wouldn't things have been easier? I create a different avatar for myself and drop him back into the scenarios that used to cause the most angst, the most friction. In this fantasy, acceptance is a given. I'm someone's son and someone's brother. Friendship with other men comes naturally. I'm welcomed into the cultural rituals and rites of passage that help make social codes more transparent, more easily assimilated on that journey into male adulthood. Who I am aligns with what others expect of me and I live into it without question.

Of course, it couldn't have happened this way. Does it ever? For anyone? Even if I hadn't struggled with the confusion that accumulated like a fog around my gender, any other fact about me—my queerness, my mixed heritage, the conservative influence of my parents' Catholicism, my sensitivity and lack of athletic talent—threatens the idea that I could have emerged from those developmental years of my life with fewer doubts about who I was or what it means to be a man.

It's easy to take a narrow view of your own story, to get hunkered down inside one point of view and assume that others haven't also struggled from their position to formulate a vision of themselves that can account for all the contradictions, aggressions, and competing desires that are at play when we, in our nascent identifications, seek belonging or safety or love.

I think that's why I've sometimes needed writers like Martin Wiley and books like this one—to pull me out of my own narrative long enough to notice how universally alienating masculinity can be, how "fed by our uncertainty."

When Did We Stop Being Cute? opens in that liminal space of adolescence, where The Woods and the playgrounds that once propagated a sense of endless possibility for Wiley and his friends become a symbol of their confinement, a minimal shelter against the boredom and violence of the White New Jersey suburbs, where "even the air // declares itself your enemy [and] joins the rest of the world in / holding you // down."

In that transition, innocence gives way to a new awareness of his racialized body—suddenly threatening to others—and the shame, rage, and capacity for self-destruction that surfaces from that shifting reality.

I hesitate to introduce Wiley's collection using the safely abstract terminology of subjectivity because his own language is much more embodied than that, much more attuned to the fist-to-flesh confrontations that "defined power" for him at that age. He writes:

> To be filled
> with such horror, such glorious
>
> violence—a dream unspoken but always
> shared. We knew the anger of course but the goal,
>
> the goal was to somehow find a way to
> maintain it, to live within it . . . & to force
> others to bear the perfect weight of it.

Blazingly honest and self-revealing, Wiley's verse doesn't reduce his experiences to a set of foregone conclusions about what it means to be young, Black, and male in America, but searches instead to parse the tangle of events that lead up to the devastating fate of a close friend and come to represent his fraught coming of age.

The poet here samples his memories just like the song lyrics he uses to retitle them, threading together a new arrangement that lets him see what he couldn't see then and understand what his younger self couldn't.

Why, for example, did the *"first time a brother / won the goddamn Homecoming King"* register as a collective triumph for people like his sister, when Nelson Mandela's release from prison hardly stirs a reaction in her at all? What made albums like *It Takes a Nation of Millions to Hold Us Back* and 2 Live Crew's *Banned in the U.S.A.* so revelatory, so life changing? What made one boy deserving of loyalty and another an easy target for petty cruelty? Which threats seemed inescapable and which ones "emerged from our own // mistakes"?

And, if the operating principle of young Martin's life back then was,

you cannot lose

if they do not know they can hurt you,
if they do not know they have hurt you,
if they do not know you,

then the poet intervenes now to admit that hurt, to allow himself to be known, and to find a more redemptive way through the impossible and bewildering demands that manhood places on us.

When I've previously been asked about my own attraction to writing poetry, I've heard myself respond that being a poet is the only identity I've ever been able to arrive at on my own terms. That feels as right a reason as any to do it. It's a maneuver, I suppose, a way to make sense of the disparate influences that make us who we are and live with the questions that have no ready answers.

What does it mean to become a man?

I don't know. I don't think Martin Wiley, even at the finish of this book, knows either. The genius and the surprise of this collection is that he doesn't have to. By writing it, he locates a voice capable of harmonizing with the unresolved and fragmented parts of his life, remixing them to make a music that is as humorously insightful as it is angry, as generous as it is serious.

I urge you to listen.

Nico Amador
September 2022

NOTE

This is an act of poetry, *not* journalism. Names have been changed, characters combined or left out, and poetic license applied liberally. The goal has been to search for "truth," not necessarily fact. To paraphrase the line from *The Man Who Shot Liberty Valance*, when the poem becomes fact, print the poem.

Martin Wiley
October 4, 2022

PART ONE

THE MINUTE THEY
SEE ME, FEAR ME

But nevertheless, I'll say it again
That these are the people that we call friends

—Whoudini,
"Friends"

Prologue: Early evening by the abandoned school

That summer ended like a rejected lyric
from some forgotten Billy Joel record, when Jimmy
    Peterson's dad was found
face down in the family pool. Pete told me
& Danny

all about it sitting on the wall by the old abandoned school
overlooking Delaware Avenue,
finishing off a pair of stolen six-packs & a bag of chips.

We watched the traffic pass,
a bored stream built from station wagons & light-blue
    hatchbacks. My radio
played softly, its slight voice full
of tiny ripples in the night,
dark & muffled beats which whispered
in a language I had already proclaimed my native tongue.

Back then, we didn't know anyone
who was dead.

So we marked it best we could: saved our last beer &
    poured it onto the crumbling
blacktop, dousing the cracks & the patches of dark
green weeds slipping through in a final flood of bubbles &
    confused
desires. Goodbye Jimmy Peterson's

dad, with your awkward belly & your endless supply of
floral pattern boxer shorts. Goodbye summer,
with your immense days & so many classified
nights. & now hello

to fall, to the rebirth of high school,
with all its continuing angers & accumulated rejections,
both the expected & the shocking. It seems you
trained us well, after all;

we almost missed you, when you were gone.

We can't afford to be innocent

Secret cigarettes tasted the best.
Spying on parents & neighbors
as they slipped into matching station wagons or each year's
slightly more expensive sedan,
or the just-turned-45 fathers as they strode into a topless
    streak of a car,

hidden in The Woods we could watch them,
& knowing they couldn't see the flames
dancing on our lips
made the burn last twice as long,
made the fire feel twice as real.

     *   *   *

I wish I could remember
I said to Pete & Danny
just when I stopped
being cute.

It was a simple truth.

Unfortunately, shifting bodies don't come equipped with
an engine light standard,
prepped to instantly flick on to warn of such looming
    transitions.

One day, adorable soft chocolate skin
morphed into something
intense, something
bitter, something
pure.

     *   *   *

The Woods across from my house ruled our minds. This
    hidden world
consisted of a one-block-long
stretch of trees just wide enough to
cover the fact that everything behind it
looked the same as anything before it,
looked the same as anything around it.
Yet that strip stood out for what it hid,
& that dead-end cul-de-sac seemed so much more alive
    because of it.

*   *   *

We cupped the ends of those cigarettes, a nifty trick we'd
    picked up in our time fighting
through the thick & deadly jungles of Vietnam

movies—I'm telling you, it was a struggle every day to survive
the endless monotony, the routine, all those deaths

that took way too long to arrive.
There was a sense of beauty within its horridness,
a meaning in their war's meaninglessness—
they, at least, knew what they were not willing to fight for.
All we knew was who our enemies were, & sometimes
    that's
not quite enough.

*   *   *

When we were little, we were certain we
were the reason for The Woods' existence, & so we
waged endless bloody remakes of the Battle of Endor,
staged sprint-sized BMX races & relished our first
    attempts at fistfights,
candy cigarettes, & bubble gum & always remained just within

Mom-shouting distance.

*   *   *

The Andersons' dog had to be avoided, if at all possible. A
    Great Dane, chained, lunging
at the cage—both of us shocked
when the bars didn't break.
That dog knew me, every time.

*   *   *

Our block held ten families, a fairly average number for the
    neighborhood, but
six were Black, the rest Irish,

a darkness held back only by
that simple strip of green.

*   *   *

We hid in tops of trees,
buried treasures under roots & leaves,
starting with a box for comic books & moving on to a
    cooler for our parents' beer &
eventually a Tupperware tightly sealed for dime bags &
    rolling papers.

*   *   *

Mrs. Anderson told me when I strolled over to walk my
    little sister home from
a playdate with their youngest
that the dog had been abused by a Black man,
a very Black man, in her words, spoken with such sorrow &
    apology,

& that was the reason why she would lose her little doggy
    mind when I came by.

I was ten, light-skinned & glasses, an unkempt afro of
    blond & brown hair full of twigs & leaves & earth, eyes
    barely reaching over the fence that separated
their endless backyard from The Woods.

A very Black man.

Such sorrow
& apology.

      *   *   *

By the time Demon Puberty worked his magic, our flesh
had long been transformed within the neighborhood's
    peeking eyes.

At 4, we were precious,
I said to Pete & Danny.
By 8, precocious.

& 10,

dangerous.

They said nothing.

Because this was not new information.

Before we reached 16, we felt the weight of it all, even as
    we denied it all,
& hid our understandings from one another.
Some things you just do.

      *   *   *

The Woods penned in our street.
Caged, like that fucking dog,
only we were never surprised when our bars didn't bend.
We said that our little world looked the same as anything
    around it, but
as always, we lied.

      *   *   *

In the interest of fairness, despite the
numerous barbecues & all the
never-ending kids' parties that filled their summers,
that packed their backyard,
that rattled her cage,
I'm pretty sure that I
was the closest thing
to "a very Black man" the poor beast ever saw.

      *   *   *

Secret cigarettes tasted the best.
Inevitably,
Mrs. Anderson or some other worried mother
would catch sight of something
moving
in The Woods,
& a bored officer would pull up, red-&-blues flashing,
    Maglite in hand
to slowly scan the trees, giving us
time to scatter
over a dog-less fence, & out
into the real world.

There ain't no need for ya

Actual 5th grade joke that received actual 5th grade laughs:

Q: *What's black & white & red all over?*
A: *Zebra after I punched him in the lip.*

This was before biracial, those days when Barry O. was known
only to his family, the times when
if someone like me tried to claim the name
African-American
they received raised eyebrows, & if they dared claim
the other half of identity they
received raised fists.

(Those fists
came painted every shade.)

I am the Zebra.
I claimed it, before it
claimed me.

But—
in the interest of full disclosure—

I didn't bleed too much when he
punched my lip
that time.

Peace is a dream (Kids in America Part One)

Pete was thin,
just muscle, dark skin, & anger,
stuffed inside an ancient Iron Maiden *The Number of the
    Beast* T-shirt.

He led us through so many
shadows & into the park
—we would have followed him anywhere—
officially it was closed for the night, but that only meant
no one would notice we were there.

Silent, we headed for the swing set, which had become,
for decades, *the* place for teenagers
out late. It was cleaned regularly
but the weeds along the fence were
a breeding ground

for broken glass,
used condoms, tiny vials,
plastic baggies. Then Pete nodded
to Danny, who pulled his grandfather's stolen flask
from his back pocket.

We drank while Pete rolled joints, the only sound
the creaking of those rusted swings.

On nights like these, when the air
teased the ability to become free & clear, when we
could spot the night sky if not
the stars, our future seemed to live & breathe
alongside us, & we could still dream
of connections
that mattered.

All alone with you makes the butterflies in me arise

Hey are you going to the prom?

she asked.

*   *   *

Rose had a habit of eating off my plate. We only got
so many fries, man, & I didn't plan on sparing any.

But she never cared.

*   *   *

What kind of fucked up Jersey town doesn't have a diner?

A place named after one of the Greek goddesses, or the
    Parthenon,
the real imaginative spots went with a random word that
    sounded Greek, like
Nikos, Anathema, or Trilogy.

*   *   *

She had a way of smiling when I was being petty. She
woke me on the phone once, actually more than once,
to argue something
I had done in her dream.

But I never minded.

*   *   *

12

If the owners of the diner were not Greek, they were Jewish.

If not Jewish,
Black.

If not Black, well,
everyone just agreed to pretend they were Greek.

    *   *****   *****

She had skin dark as mine, somewhere my mix met
her tan. She took me down
the shore & though she held my hand I
could never keep my eyes from straying to her bikini.

But she never let on she noticed.

    *   *****   *****

Diners littered every highway, crossroad, backwoods, train
   stop.

But we worked at the local Friendly's, which was
—it pains me to say—the closest we had. Pocket cash,
foodfights, whippets, flirting—on Saturdays the manager
wasn't in & we closed the place ourselves—
vodka milkshakes & triple-decker sandwiches.
A great place to work. Until it dawned on me
all the white guys gave orders & wore white shirts,
all the white girls took orders & wore short skirts, &
guys like me were

hidden
in the back, roasting
over the grill or steaming
our faces beside the dishwasher.

You'd be surprised how long it can take a teenager to
    realize
perfectly obvious shit like that.

& we still didn't have a diner.

*   *   *

She had a way of not-crying when
some idiot broke her heart. I hated
all of her boyfriends on sight, on sound, even
on smell.

What I hated most
was when I was proven right.

But she never held it against me.

*   *   *

I watched her by a table of
sophomores, wiping the floor,
doing her best to ignore their eyes dropping
down her shirt. She stood, flashed me a smile,
& disappeared

behind the partition that hid
the grill from the customers.
She came around the corner, with a giggle.

Hey are you going to prom?

Rose, it's October.
I haven't given it much thought.

*   *   *

There is a moment of panic when
your best-friend-total-crush actually notices you
& you're not sure what it means.

Everything sweats,
& you just hold your breath
to wait for your heart to cease pounding.

Eventually you realize it never stops.

*   *   *

Well?

Rose,
I said,
I can't think that far ahead.

She giggled.
You can't think past five minutes ago.

Well,
I said, thinking quickly,
*whatever, just save the last dance
for the Zebra,*

& she

smiled.

Kind hearts don't make a new story
(Kids in America Part Two)

Colors,
Danny said,

I'ma see that movie
like 20 times. My dad reads his Bible
every night.

We
stared at him.

    *   *****   *****

It is a difficult thing,
with today's eyes, to see
the way our suburban selves used to view those
gangs of L.A.

    *   *****   *****

That book don't change, Danny said. *But he*
studies it, like he's worried

someone rewrote a bunch of shit
when he wasn't looking.

Oh, but that's different, said Jimmy Peterson.

I mean, it is the Bible.

Right?

Something like a phenomenon

The story I heard was rookie slugger Darryl Strawberry
    asked veteran
& soon-to-be legend
Keith Hernandez how to deal with a
hitting slump.

Hernandez laid out a line of coke & said,
Hit that. Then you can't miss, every time.

    *   *****   *****

As soon as I woke the radio
went on. Sunday morning, the 12th of February.
I stayed in my room, as there was nowhere
interesting to go. That year I was grounded more than free,
life contained in my room while TV became
a random visitor never allowed to stay for long.

I switched from WBLS to WFAN, from
Black music to American sports. Sunday morning,
not a time for hip hop, or so
radio proclaimed. But as the dial slipped

from one well-worn groove to another, something caught,
threw me off simply by existing, out of
place, incorrect. No
context.

    *   *****   *****

Lawrence Taylor of our minds, we acted out
that hit! on a daily basis, becoming those 237 pounds of
    righteous fury

landing in that sickening crack on Joe Theismann's right
leg. Did LT know, even then, that Joe's career was fractured,
splintered, never to heal—is that why
he leaped to his feet, screamed to the sidelines?

That defined power, to us. To be filled
with such horror, such glorious

violence—a dream unspoken but always
shared. We knew the anger of course but the goal,

the goal was to somehow find a way to
maintain it, to live within it, to be LT & to force
others to bear the perfect weight of it.

*   *   *

I didn't know the voice on the radio, at first listen. But I
 could guess.

It was the accent that clued me in—one rarely heard
on these airwaves. Not too long ago our class had been
 dragged to see *Cry Freedom*,
& you never forget any movie that gets
you out of school. & then *Lethal Weapon 2*

trained me in the art
of White & Black South African voices, with
one to fear, & one to fear for.

This voice was steady, continuous, not a sound bite
 signaling
the station's noble intentions never actually intended to be
 acted upon.
This was a speech, uninterrupted, & wars have to be
 declared

for presidents to get that kind of airtime.

There was only ever one possible speaker, & his
    impossibility made
his inevitability.

*   *   *

Michael Spinks may have been the most frightened
    human.
To his credit, he ducked down, slid through the ropes,
slipped off his robe, stood in his corner,
waited.

There was no fight to come, only a beating
hovering over us all, delayed.

We fantasized of looking to someone, anyone, & seeing

Michael Spinks's eyes failing to look back.

*   *   *

I did not understand what I was hearing.

& then, back to the studio, where some
milk White reporter with practiced lack of passion
said what I clearly knew, but didn't dare believe:

Nelson Mandela, free.

*   *   *

The stadium was full. Dwight Gooden's return
from drug rehab. We heard the roar
as he took the mound & we quickened our steps,
muscled through the security,

paused on the stairs to catch that curveball breaking
past Barry Bonds who turned &
sadly took his seat as we

screamed
into ours.

*   *   *

Out of my room. Stumble around. Find someone. Anyone.
  There. My sister, sprawled on her bed, door to her room
  open, cutting pictures from a magazine, Top 40 soft on
  her radio.

Did you hear?
I said,
I can't believe it, I mean, I never thought—

Yeah, yeah,
she said, eyes on her magazine,
I know. Mike Tyson lost.

No,
I said.
I mean did you hear—
wait, what?

*   *   *

It was the fumbling for the mouthpiece that I remember.
Goliath, reaching for the broken haft of his spear.

We watched the replay like
Philistines immobilized
in newly discovered fear, like

Grendel's baby brother hearing far-off reports
of inconceivable Death.

*   *   *

No,
I said,
Mandela. Mandela's free. He's out!

Oh,
my sister said, & flipped a page.
Ooo that's a good one, & the scissors danced around Bobby
    Brown, dropping him down
onto the bed beside her.

I stared at her.

*   *   *

(White lines) Visions, dreams of passion
(Blowing through my mind) & all the while I think of you . . .

*   *   *

You done?
she said.

Yeah,
I said,
yeah, guess I am.

Forever's gonna start tonight
(Kids in America Part Three)

Our hearts were still
throwing blows in a celluloid city across the continent. We
   nibbled popcorn we'd been too
amped to eat. There are times
when even the air

declares itself your enemy, when it
joins the rest
of the world in
holding you

down. In Jersey, we called those times *summer*.

     *   *****   *****

Well,
said Pete,
continuing the earlier conversation,

*everybody's gotta
believe in something.*

Yeah, I said.
It doesn't have to be a Bible.

Danny thought on this.

Can I just watch my gangster movie again?

Pete shrugged.

Then:
Sure,

I said.

Better to believe in Ice-T than like,
I dunno,
Jesus or Reagan or Springsteen or some shit.

Now they
all stared at me.

Yo Zebra, said Pete,

fuck *Bruce Springsteen*.

Jimmy Got Nothin' made himself a name
(Kids in America Part Four)

Pete stood & walked away from the
swings. He wiped hair from his
eyes & grasped Jimmy Peterson's
arm, & pulled him back
from the fence. We all spread out, soundless. I
looked at Danny who stuck out
his fist & I
touched mine to it,
gently.

Jimmy Peterson
took a deep breath, balled up his
fists, &
waited.

My colors beside me, I said,
one soldier stand tall.

Ready? said Pete.
Silence.

Jimmy Peterson
turned to us,

we nodded.

Then we were on him. Arms flying, fists rained from every
    direction,
a hush as we moved, the sound
of our hands & feet connecting

with Jimmy Peterson
was dull, muted, as if the air pushing

down

on us kept anyone else from hearing. Jimmy Peterson
scrambled & ducked but made
no attempts to run, got knocked down &
rolled back to his feet, again
& again. But always,

that silence.

If I could find a souvenir just to prove the world was here (Kids in America Part Five)

Okay, said Pete, *enough*.

There were tears in Jimmy Peterson's
eyes, but they held,

not daring to interrupt his
moment.

I put my arms around
him, tight. From me
to Danny, then finally

to Pete. Jimmy Peterson
spat, dark & ugly
in the light of the streetlamps,

then stretched, rolled his shoulders,

turned to us.

Alright, you motherfuckers, said Jimmy Peterson,

who's next?

After: math

Mondays were a horror when
you were a blackout.

Everyone was mad &
no one told you why.

Your left elbow hurt. But
no one told you why.

Your right sneaker: torn.
No one told you why.

In the hallway, someone would always laugh, & point.
You never got the joke.

High school was one long stupid punch line you
drank to forget.

You understood the irony. You
were always too pissed to give a fuck.

PART TWO

HEY KID,
WALK STRAIGHT,
MASTER YOUR HIGH

Oh, baby, this town rips the bones from your back

—Bruce Springsteen,
"Born to Run"

Prologue: Late night by the abandoned school

The funeral was, fittingly enough, the beginning
of the end. Rose called with

all the details; she knew I could not
be there, but I still

cared—a little. Jimmy Peterson's
dad managed to turn out quite the crowd

for what seemed to be a surprisingly
somber affair, especially considering that our limited

understanding of the right way to mark an Irish death
required a lot more tear-fueled

brawling than the family apparently had
planned for. Later Danny & I sat

alone up on that hill & after awhile I asked
if he'd known beforehand what was going to happen &

Danny took a swig off his bottle &
offered it to me. When I passed,

he swallowed his surprise & laughed,
drank more, then just shook his head. I figured he

meant it, because if Danny really knew what Pete was
    planning
there's no way he wouldn't have joined in. Rose told me

Pete arrived at the end of the afternoon, as they were
    preparing the family

to head to a nearby cousin's house—nice place, smaller
   than Jimmy Peterson's,

but better than accidentally catching a glimpse of the
   backyard pool
where it happened. & Pete strolled in, calm as you please,
   clad only

in a brand-new pair of floral-patterned boxer shorts,
purchased for the occasion. Pete shouted & offered

a beer for a toast but only spit out
a few words before he was taken down,

lifted up, taken out. The shock was probably what hit
him hardest; Pete had been forced to search far & wide &

spent more than he expected to find
the exact brand Jimmy Peterson's

dad always wore; I think they were only available at this
handmade-only tailor's shop in a tiny backroom somewhere

in The City. Even if no one else did,
Danny & I agreed Jimmy Peterson

should have known Pete meant only a
show of respect. So now Danny & I sat by ourselves &
   talked about nothing which

can be a pretty fucking interesting subject if
you approach it right & he never

offered the bottle again, which I appreciated, as we
knew I was only so strong, & so we sat until eventually

the sun rose & the night
ended & we both

wandered
off.

Look right through me, look right through me

They cornered me between my locker &   the
    roaring river
of students   Danny slipped away & left me   god I
    envied him   the camera

somehow steady throughout the rush   this Eye of
    Sauron taking it all in   I was the only one who
              flinched   backed into rusted metal
    & a newly taped photo of Sheila E.

Written along the side of the camera: "Property of Scotch
    Plains-Fanwood High School, Tech Dept."

The microphone danced in her hand   hypnotic
    cautious   constant

Written at the top of the microphone: "SPF News"

She was so blond   I no longer see her face   all I recall is
    so much yellow hair
a perky sun of curls that lit up the corridor

SPF News

                                        How does it feel,

    she said,

& her voice—her voice!   sweetness forged into a
    weapon   happiness
    a battle flag

Tell us, how does it feel, she asked   *to be back here at* Spiffy
   High?

My response   which was the only *possible* response
   was judged
      inappropriate   for public-access news.

Glory Days (Jersey Verse Part One)

Springsteen
was a legend to most, but he never meant sh--
to me, you see the straight-up racists were quick
to claim

the man & his name. Growing up
Jersey meant growing up within
his shadow, underneath
the deadly serious weight of *so many* songs.

Pete & I were caught,
once,
at night,
weaving down an empty hill on our way back
from the home of twin sisters too enamored to notice
they were hopelessly out of our league. A movie theater near
the bottom of their hill played all the latest hits,
my sister dropped us off there.

The twins had bribed us to make the trek
out of town & up the road to their ridiculous house
with the promise of free-reign over their parents'
    enormous
(& constantly refilled)
liquor cabinet; we were just smart enough
to keep our mouths shut
& not let them see that we
would have braved entire mountain ranges for a few deep
    kisses
& the chance (however slight) of a hand
roaming free beneath
the latest mall-bought designer blouse.

As we went down that hill, I looked around & said:
I have literally never seen so many fucking trees.

Pete was like,
I know, right? Got some big-ass houses
here, but can't even spot
them from the road.

There may have been a moon—I can't remember.
Pete passed me the Pepsi bottle, which Tina
had cleaned & expertly filled with a triple-sized martini to go,
shaken, of course, not stirred.

The first thing we heard was the music:

Born down in a dead man's town,
first kick I took was when I hit the ground.

* * *

The thing about corny sayings
is not that they are sometimes true, but
they're the only way some people can relay truths to
    others.

They *call it rap, I say we call it crap.*
This from my manager as we closed for the night.
He had come in once, on his day off, to pick up
    meaningless
papers that required his meaningless attention & found
    Rose & me
& the whole gang, to his horror, dancing
while we worked.
Understand—we did this every night & the work
always got done—he just wasn't around to see it. But now
    he decided

it was his personal managerial responsibility
to protect our growing minds from the dangers of Biz
    Markie & Digital Underground.
I still wonder how he would have reacted if
he'd arrived 20 minutes later, during the scheduled
    gangsta hour.

So, now he showed up every night,
stacks of CDs in each hand, to play DJ for teenagers
who could not have hated him more if he'd been a cop.
We laughed in his face when he played the Stones, staged a
    sit-in
when he tried the Beatles, & none of us liked to talk about
    what happened
the Night of the Doors Tape.

But he would not allow *any* nonsense
when The Boss was on.
Now this, he would say,
leaning back in his booth &
sipping his Diet Coke,
this is real *music*.

*   *   *

The music. Then the headlights.

What you had to notice about pickup trucks,
when spotted in a wealthy neighborhood like this,
was the dirt, or the lack thereof. A truck
with dust or better yet
with mud was probably safe. There might even be
brothers in it, or Mexicans
(which was close enough in the suburbs),
there to take care of some rich lady's lawn.

But if you could see that truck gleam
in what little light streaked
through the curtain of leaves,

son, keep
your damn
guard
up.

* * *

Rumor was that there was a push by local activists
(& politicians trying to get their votes)
to make "Born to Run" the official state song of New Jersey.

I'm just gonna let that sink in for a moment.

* * *

We ducked to the side of the road, but
those highbeams lit us up like
convicts trying to escape in one of those old black-&-white
    prison movies.
The bottles of Bud came next, & their choice of brew said
    everything.
The bottles, you see, were half-full, & anyone
who throws bottles with beer still in them
can afford to drink better beer than Budweiser.

U-S-A! U-S-A! U-S-A!

Blood & beer do not mix well
when they both are running down
into your eyes.

U-S-A! U-S-A! U-S-A!

Thanks for the reminder,
said Pete,
but we know where the fuck we at.

*   *   *

True fact: there remain
a dozen hairstyles
that only survive

at the Jersey shore.

*   *   *

Five sat in the cargo bed,
who knows how many in the cab;
dude in the passenger seat fancied himself the leader & had
questions for us but I couldn't make them out over the
screaming:

*Born
in the USA!
I was
booorn
in the USA, now!*

& of course, the constant shouts of
Nigger go home! from the boys in the back.

I snatched up a broken bottle
& Pete grabbed a fallen branch, then
helped me to stand, &
we faced them, as best we could. We were under
no delusions that we could win, or even survive, but we
made it *very* clear to them
that neither of us had any intentions of

going down alone.

      *   *   *

I don't think I really understood Malcolm X
until this quote:

*Stop talking
'bout the South.
As long as you south
of the Canadian border,*

you South.

      *   *   *

The song ended.
The driver peeled off, spraying
pebbles & shards of glass into our faces.
We covered, at least we tried to.

Laughter like theirs always echoes.

Once they were gone we
washed our injuries
with the remnants of our martinis, which we thought
was pretty a badass way to sterilize a wound, & used
what was left of my shirt
to slow the bleeding.

C'mon Zebra, said Pete,
get a move on.

Your sister's gonna be waiting.

We Are the Champions (Jersey Verse Part Two)

We won, she said,
throwing open my door & leaning in.

We won, we won!

* * *

It was the year my sister was Puerto Rican. Or
faux-Rican, if you will.

Gold hoops dangled from ears, dark purple lipstick,
miniskirts pushed out her ass,
two-inch-long fingernails, flame red,
& just barely enough high-school Spanish to
fake an accent.
A gorgeous mess of a brilliant disguise, much more insult
    than inspiration,
but she was fully aware that the few Latinas in our
    neighborhood had far too many
actual problems to care about her.

The year before she'd been Italian, & before that
Jewish, mainly for the mitzvahs.
More than one white-haired old bubbeh
held out hope her grandson
would finally catch the attention
of that sweet Ashkenazi girl with the large brown eyes.

(Before Obama, we all dealt with being mixed in different
    ways.)

* * *

We are the champions, my friend . . .

She stood in my doorway,
waited for me to join in, as listeners usually do
when that song is sung.

no time for losers . . .

    *   *   *

I waited for a pause in the song & said,
*Why are you still home? Don't you have a date waiting for you
to come dancing or something?*

Then giant brown eyes danced into my room in a way my
    angst-ridden green ones
never could.

She hugged me
& I froze.

We won,
she repeated,
softer this time,
& I could only nod, &

wait.

    *   *   *

My sister had the brownest eyes,
thick, triumphant,

she had eyes that knew she was the oldest, that she was
    always right,
that things would all work out precisely the way she told
    them to.

Her eyes had a gravitational pull astronauts could train in.

Yet, they were always able
to silently calm a baby brother
who crept to her door
because nightmares woke him,

who crept to her door
because he couldn't go to their mother's,
because they both knew their mother was the one he'd
   been dreaming about.

      *   *   *

Darryl,
my sister said
& squeezed tight.

Darryl who?
I said.

Darryl motherfucking Homecoming King,
she said.

I was fairly certain I understood all those words yet
that sentence didn't make any sense.

Darryl—that name again!—
Darryl's the new Homecoming King!

The first time a brother
won the goddamn Homecoming King!

      *   *   *

I don't know
if you yourself are aware of this but

the popular kids,

they had weird issues.

* * *

She took my silence
for celebration, &

spun me around, & we
danced to Queen, & she

pulled me out of my exile & into
a truce

that neither of us believed
would last the week but

it was one we both knew

mattered,
all the same.

Past the days of yes y'allin'
(Jersey Verse Part Three)

It was 2 Live Crew, of course, that taught me
it was actually okay to like
Bruce Springsteen.

    *   *   *

Fighting against the current on the way to
second-period biology, I felt a quick tug. Pete had snagged
my arm but he shouldn't have been there, everyone knew
he never missed history on the other side
of the school—yet there he was, waiting.
In his hand: a tape.

There was a power, once, in tapes.

Battered, worn, outer shell scratched, faded, yet the word
Megadeth remained, clear as day. He
held it out to me. I preferred
not to be rude, to a friend. But,
you know, Megadeth.

I wasn't really looking to listen to regular death, so
this was a little much.

Yo, man,
you gotta *hear this.*

    *   *   *

The right to be angry is the most American thing anyone
    can claim.
Everything else is born from that. It is the very reason we
    want our guns

or speech protected. More than
a flag, more than a song, this
is what brings us together, what makes us one.

Get down for the prophets of rage.

     *   *****   *****

Pete thrust that tape into my hands &
I could see those little tabs at the top
had been pierced, ruptured,
conquered.

What is it?

He only shook his head,
& just like that, he was gone.

Clear the way for the prophets of rage.

     *   *****   *****

In the summer of 1990, three members of
2 Live Crew were pulled
off stage & arrested as they played at a sex club.

Officially, they were charged with obscenity for music
    performed at a sex club.

That may be the greatest sentence I will ever write.

     *   *****   *****

When I finally got around to homework that evening, I
    threw Pete's
tape on, figuring if I'm already doing algebra,
ain't no tape gonna make it any worse.

No work got done that night.

It Takes a Nation of Millions.

The music was like bug repellant for parents, a screeching whine
that repeated, endlessly, effortlessly, the loop
was the meaning, the meaning was in the loop. I mean, the album started

with a goddamn air-raid siren, a warning, a call
& response that flicked something buried
within cultural DNA.

It's like that, I'm like Nat leave me the hell alone
If you don't think I'm a brother—check the chromosomes.

* * *

It is an inconvenient truth
that free speech can be attacked on all sides, when a right-wing Florida DA
locked arms with a Democratic soon-to-be vice president's wife

to lock up some Black dudes
for singing about butts. The surreality of
strange bedfellows goes both ways, however,

& in July 1990 2 Live Crew released *Banned in the U.S.A.,* notable
as the first album to come equipped
with a parental advisory sticker.

You have to understand, the title track
drove White people in Jersey fucking insane.

* * *

I played Pete's tape, flipped it,
played it, the loop was the meaning,

the meaning was hidden in the loop.

(Stereo, stereo) describes my scenario.

* * *

You see, this was Bruce,
the poet of the Parkway, the god whose words united
Wall Street commuters with Meadowlands tailgaters,
who traced a sacred lineage from Dylan all the way back
to Whitman, but better, more real
than either of them could hope to be.
A man of the people.

& we all knew which people.

My friends & I basked in the outrage of all those who
screamed their love for Jersey Jesus, &
shrieked their horror that some no-talent Blacks
had taken sacred tracks
& turned them into some weird anti-American defense
of perversion. Finally, we thought, the music of the people

who refused to hire us,
who labeled me Zebra or half-breed,
who didn't bother to hide their disbelief when we aced
    math tests,
who assumed we cheated when we bested their kid's SAT
    scores,

for once the music of the people
who hated everything about us
would be used to speak for us.

*   *   *

& then,
Kurt Loder, *MTV News*,
interrupting *Yo! MTV Raps* to report on the controversy,

read a statement from
The Boss himself:

Anyone who doesn't support
2 Live Crew's use of "Born in the U.S.A."
obviously never listened to
the lyrics of my song, anyway.

*   *   *

In those days, MTV still played music,
& when
the time allotted to hip hop was over,
they went straight to the video,
Bruce,
in concert,

Born in the U.S.A.

& for the very first time,

my friends & I
actually listened.

We're all ice cream castles in the summertime

Pete told me he had a few minutes left cleaning up & then
we could punch out, so Rose & I practiced
flirting while doing our best to ignore the
never-ending Kenny G monstrosity streaming over
the speakers when a large party stumbled through the
    door & up
to the ice cream counter & Jimmy Peterson
was in the center of them &
there Bonnie was, caught
by his hand.

     *   *****   *****

Bonnie had danced for the world our last night together,
even with her up on stage I
could see us in her eyes, in her motions. Until the
music ended & she fell

into my arms, without breath, without weight, that smile
slapped me & without thinking I
pulled her so tight to me it didn't hurt. But then
I was forced to remember we
weren't alone.

     *   *****   *****

She was more blond than I remembered, & skinny, I guess.
The thing to keep in mind, as I watched her,
was how much Bonnie hated being alone. I knew that,
I even understood that, it was just
looking at her now I so desperately wished she
could find somewhere else to be
not-alone.

51

My hands, resting on the table in front of me, open, empty.
The skin: shredded, wrinkled. A pattern

of fading nicks & cuts & burns from the dishwasher & grill
danced alongside my lifeline. & under my left eye

that final bruise was still visible, though faint, & it
throbbed
slightly, not willing to be forgotten.

Rose tried to get my attention. I could not control my eyes.
Pete
was laughing as he emerged from the back, drying
hands on a grimy overused towel. He stopped, frozen

in an instant hate. Spotting him, Bonnie waved
& slowly he grinned,
more display of teeth
than sign of happiness.

*　*　*

Each year, when the seasons changed, Pete was fired. The
manager,
fed up with drunken arrivals & disrespectful exits, would
have stern words & a sharp dismissal, then sit in his booth
& angrily reflect on all that he'd done to make it work *this*
time, &
tell anyone who would listen that finally he
found someone better on the grill than Pete.

It would usually last about two weeks, no more than three,
before waitresses would threaten a strike
& the manager would struggle through four or five
scream-filled dinner hours
& eventually a strategic slowdown from the boys in the back

would lead to Pete's inevitable return,
unapologetic & with some additional monetary incentives,
    which always
went to a few bottles to be passed around as soon as the
    boss wasn't looking.

*   *   *

Bonnie tried to smile at me
across all those miles & miles between us but
it didn't really take.

I could feel a restaurant full of eyes hover over me,
    searching
for my response to this new knowledge: Jimmy Peterson,
dating my girl. But that's only
because they solely saw the world
as made up from things they could look to own. She was never
my girl—just not how things work, really.
No. What got me was knowing
that when we broke up, we both broke

apart & I guess some guys look for that in a girl & in the end
that's why I could not forgive him. Now, she stood there,
    almost lost
in his shadow, though Jimmy Peterson
was never all that big.

*   *   *

Those smiles of hers always started trouble.
The first was a waiting smile delivered at precisely the
    wrong time,
which of course stole my heart, & the closing one a
    truthful smile

given at a moment when we desperately needed lies. Her
    parents had passed
a decade before & now all
she had was five angry Italian brothers, & all
they had was watching out for her. When she
came off stage
her glow was for me, & that,
that didn't go over so well.

*   *   *

I found myself wondering if her brothers liked
    Jimmy Peterson.
Probably. He was the type they'd have picked out for her.
    Which was
kind of funny, when I thought about it.

Well. Maybe when someone else thought about it.

*   *   *

The hold on her hand was firm & for the first time I
realized how well Jimmy Peterson
wore that bland Whiteness

only Americans possess, the kind built
from pieces of everything, yet manages

to stare back
to nothing.

*   *   *

Rose called my name as I walked out &
I paused, gave the best face I could. She started
toward me but some overwrought soccer mom squealed

for more juice for little Davey & just like that she
was pulled away. I blew through the door &
into the foyer & out the exit &

down the stairs. Sweat on my cheeks & the air
was cool, I could feel wind
on my face, light & steady, mixing with my
sweat as if someone were kissing my
forehead. The trees along the edges of
the parking lot & by the sidewalk rustled softly, leaves
    dancing, as if
like us immortal.

I looked out at the street. It always made me feel
so tiny. Main Street.
Maybe ten cars at its busiest & this
was where the nightlife lived,
two or three bars (why count when they'd never let me in?),
a bunch of pretentious restaurants, & this
wanna-be diner. & yet, this was all
we had, all that we were.

You got a smoke?
asked Pete from behind me. I offered him one.

We walked.

You know what the worst of it is?
he said.

I waited.

Pretty sure that girl loved you.

Now he waited. I shrugged.

Yeah, well,
I said,

it's pretty to think so,
I guess.

A self-made monster

We began that Friday playing after-dark Wiffle ball in
Danny's backyard. He had just installed tiny spotlights
    hanging
from branches so all night we could fight & curse every

pitch & when eventually we got tired we sat on
faded lawn chairs & talked & drank until 10 when
his parents were due. No stars & the moon mostly hid but

the sky reflected back the energy of the world until even
the shadows under the trees seemed
sort of eerie & bright.

     *   *****   *****

We argued Sonny Crockett versus John McClane,
Yankees versus Mets, an overhand right versus
the sucker punch, & whether or not

unshaven scruff should count as a beard. Then
scanned through *The New York Times* to pick arguments
completely by chance & randomly swapped sides

without thought or the slightest hint
of bitterness or betrayal; for us,
it was the embrace of conflict that mattered.

     *   *****   *****

On the streets we relied
on Pete's Spidey-sense for warnings;

it had never failed us, not once. A radar detector
for the darker skinned, it

screamed
the moment before the siren

sounded, the second before
searchlights rounded corners, before

the cruiser slipped between parked cars to roam,
   one last attempt to scare out late-night prey. We

did not yet know of threats that emerged from our own

mistakes, that not all dangers
came clothed in blue, & we

had no names, then, for these things we
were learning, feeling

inside ourselves, for these
horrors

being born
so deep within us.

     *   *   *

Waded through streets grown wide &
dark & full, where houses buried
themselves behind forests of

well-manicured trees & perfectly shaped
shrubs, the only sound to scuff the silence just
the slapping of sneakers against newly poured sidewalks.

     *   *   *

We bore with us the demands of man,

of men, the dread contained in deference to elders & love
    for big brothers,

the disgust of respect earned from bullies & bullshitters,
the fear of fathers & the frightening hope that

someday
we would become them.

*   *   *

It was Danny who noticed first, a slim figure moving
quickly down the hill, concealed by
shadows & dancing leaves, &

Danny nudged Pete,
said only two words:
Jimmy Peterson.

We didn't actually need light to see him, his
bouncing stride spoke
as clearly as a photo. It was obvious he

had spotted us & was making as quick an exit
as he could, though Jimmy Peterson
always had to swing, just a little, when he walked.

*   *   *

The shame
of actions taken when you didn't

know better, when you should have known
better, & when you

should have known

you should have been better,

actions like these leave scars that we
pick at to find they pick back, wounds that

remind us manhood is never a given, but
neither is it an option. It is not marked

on our flesh nor grown on
outsides of bodies; to be

the man you have to beat
the man

hiding within you, a stranger planted
like poisonous seeds, sprouted

from music we listen to, movies we devour, &

countless heroes we didn't know
were never deserving of our faith.

These legends, these lies, these
myths

blossomed in our souls, fed by our uncertainty &
the paralyzing panic that we would not

fit in & the degrading
horror

of knowing that sometimes
we would.

*　*　*

Pete knelt, then sprang back up with a determined grin &

whispered,

Fuck you,
Jimmy Peterson,

& bounced a rock in his hand once twice
to get its weight, & let it

fly. We watched it sail, our calm
certain first-strike Peacekeeper missile whistling so softly,
   landing

with the faintest barely heard thud right
on Jimmy Peterson's

back, drawing out a groan we
could actually hear, staggering him, & Jimmy Peterson

ran off down the hill, steady pace, no swing left
in his step. & we

could only
laugh.

Yeah they do it all the time

My father came to me &
I could see myself so heavy
on him, he always seemed to carry me

with him
throughout the house.

Your mother & I have decided,
he said,
you should talk to a psychiatrist.
We think you need help.

He waited. Are oaks
that determined before
the hurricane, when they first

start to sense hard winds
coming? Do they hold
rage in place like a father? Do they lean

toward the wind as if daring it to begin?

What about me?
I asked.
What about what I think?

He gave me his office look, the calm bland fierceness
of a Black face prepared
through decades climbing corporate ladders, delivering
   smiling

suggestions that somehow found ways
to land harder than orders—in those days, secretaries & sons
were more closely related than either of us cared to admit.

Well,
he said,
in a slow rolling voice
expertly designed
to convey the sincerest desire to know,

we want to hear what you think.

I said,
I think I don't want to,
I think I shouldn't have to.

He nodded.

Your mother & I
feel you should.

With that, he was gone.

Swallowed screams stick in your throat like
nothing else can.

My father was built to stand firm
in the face of my loudest scream,
my hardest wind,

& unlike oaks, he possessed the ability
to knock the wind out of whoever dared scream twice at him.
I lay in bed, trembling & cold,
too choked to sleep—
frustration serves up the best insomnia.

You must understand—I could not lose.

My entire belief in myself,
a belief growing & bubbling in layers & levels that I
was just beginning to suspect,
this belief was able to build itself only on
what I was not—
& I was not someone who lost.

I thought,
They can't make me talk to anyone.
You can lead a horse to water but

you cannot compel him
to discuss his thirst.

Not one sound not one grunt not one whisper no
tears no yells no insights no dreams no
peeks at inner depths or glances
at hidden thoughts. I forged
my own face of calm bland fierceness
in that furious endless sleepless night.

I have built myself only
from what I am not.

I did not speak,
I did not lose,
& my belief in
myself was firmly constructed by this,
the most masculine of myths:
you cannot lose

if they do not know they can hurt you,
if they do not know they have hurt you,
if they do not know you.

Unruly boys who will not grow up

It was always such a beautiful sight to us.
This school, not ours but we could dream,
silenced, lying here

defeated, dead, no more danger than a discarded matchbox
    or
an absent parent. We could not put in words

the longing, the hope
that it immediately sparked within us—

this too, it whispered,
this too shall pass.

     *   *   *

By now the booze
was warm, but when you relied on the kindness of
    strangers (& older siblings),
you drank what you got.

     *   *   *

The car screamed up in the dark, drove off
the parking lot & over the grass that crept up to the
    crumbling front door &

even Pete didn't sense its approach & when
the headlights pounced,

they pinned us where we sat, instant &
insistent. We blinked, listening

to the crash of doors flinging themselves open

before offended tires had even finished
furious squealing.

* * *

Oh shit,
said Danny,

it's Jimmy Peterson.

* * *

There are some mistakes
that fester, that bear only
more pain.

* * *

Shadows sprang from the lights, Jimmy Peterson
the smaller of the two. His father, as always clad only
in those damn floral-patterned boxers,
slammed his door & was on me quicker
than I would have guessed possible.

Well?
he said,

you just a pussy when my son's not alone?

The words spat
from his lips, as if

just having to let them touch his tongue filled him
with disgust.

Dad I—

You shut up,
he said,
without a glance in his son's direction.

His eyes were locked on me, all that contempt poured
like a well-trained volcano, like long-diverted floodwaters,

those eyes were small & iron & flared brighter than
the headlights still trained upon us.

We didn't mean anything,
said Danny.
We were just messing around.

He was ignored.

You ready?
he said,
& for the first time looked to his son. But Jimmy Peterson

was focused only on me, & while his eyes
did not sit as solid as his father's, I

could still feel them
even in the dark.

* * *

Children,
said James Baldwin,
*have never been very good
at listening to their elders, but*

*they have never failed
to imitate them.*

* * *

From the corner of my eye I could see Danny, his face
as shocked & lost
as I felt. I turned to him but
then the world shook, stars appeared
for a second, then
died.

Sucker-punch.

Shook my head clear & first thing I saw was
those damn boxers, then lifted
my eyes to see Jimmy Peterson.

Between father & son their bitter thick unspoken war
    claimed the air,
my own conflicts with Jimmy Peterson

dwarfed by this
revelation, this
revulsion, this
self-loathing.

My jaw throbbed & all I knew was the pounding pounding
    pounding
of my pulse & that beat was a horror & every inch cell
    muscle roared its own
song & I could feel

my mind

as it filled with image after image after image of men
    standing before me,
all these men, ages & ages

of glaring White men. Some I knew or would know & loved
    or hated or
ignored or forgot but they all knew me,

they would never let me be
anything but what I was.

My body floated from me, all was red
& ending, all I could know was the scream

that tore loose from my lungs & poured itself
over everything, coating it in my blood my anger my soul,
    until

all was pushed aside, until the world
was dark & thick with hate.

Until, finally,
my sight gradually
came back. The scream was
still there but I could feel
the hatred dissolve, eat itself up, the world was
reborn & in that freshness of return
I realized
the scream was now solely
the property of
Jimmy Peterson.

My hands were on his head,
in his hair,
his head was the drumbeat, banging
on the hood of the car, his blood
the red. His father
watched.

       *   *   *

& once again I wished
I could remember
when I stopped being cute.

69

*　*　*

Without a sound Danny carefully helped Jimmy Peterson
to his feet. Danny's eyes hurled

such unspeakable curses at Jimmy Peterson's
father, at his own father, at a world filled with fathers.

A hand seized mine, shook it.

You might be
a real man someday, not another little bitch.

& then I felt Pete's hand, softly touching
my shoulder, & it all fell from me,

a short lifetime's worth of despair & disgust shattered
at my feet, burrowed in those cracks in the blacktop.

Jimmy, shake the man's hand.

I stuck my hand out blindly, I didn't want to have to look at
    him,
for him to now feel my eyes on him. He took my hand,
    dropped it quickly.

Let's go.

Danny went to the passenger side, opened the door. &
    Jimmy Peterson
looked up, looked at me, for a moment. His eyes
were soft & pulled me in &
we stood there, animals
trapped in a net we had been forced to see
was not the one that we had actually made.

Then he was gone.

* * *

The taste was thick, harsh, already familiar, rushing
into me. It splashed, a liquid that burned everything it
   encountered
on its way down.

It's all fucked,
I said,
& Pete & Danny agreed.

After: shock

It is the soreness of knuckles that reminds you
of the fight, & it is the relative numbness of your face
that reminds you who won.

It is the blood in your eyes that reminds you
what you did to forget, & it is the unsteadiness of your steps
that reminds you how hard you had to work.

It is the afternoon that tells you of the night & in the end,
it is this afternoon of that next day you
will never let yourself forget.

It is the bizarre realization, arriving with sudden
clarity, that despite all evidence
to the contrary, this

is finally that first day
you woke up sober.

PART THREE

BUT LIFE IS JUST A PARTY & PARTIES WEREN'T MEANT TO LAST

Death is everywhere—
There are flies on the windscreen for a start . . .

—Depeche Mode,
"Fly on the Windscreen"

Prologue: Early morning by the abandoned school

We didn't bother with beer; there was no way
to keep it cold, & bottles, like responsibilities, have ways
of piling up.

The old school had died again, a second death spawned
by the slow withering of funding, trapping it in a rotting
    chrysalis,
no condos to emerge from its shell.

The window of what I think had been a kindergarten
was the easiest to force open, & so we left all before it,
our altar of cruddy glass & rusted steel.

A few sandwiches, along with bread
& peanut butter. Some granola,
a couple large & almost sweet early apples,
two bottles of water,

& a huge packet of Reese's Pieces, mostly because
we knew how badly E.T. had freaked Pete out when we
    were little,
& these days, we could all use a good laugh.

Danny, being more practical, brought toilet paper, a few
    shirts,
a *Penthouse*, & a large flask full of his mom's whiskey.

Danny & I didn't expect to see him. I'm not sure what we
    could have done,
had we seen him. Once things have happened, there's not
    always

a return
to the beginning, or even to the good parts
in the middle.

Back then, we didn't know anyone
who had killed someone.

More than anything, I just wished I
had something to say. But there was
nothing. I missed him, that was true, but
that had been going on long before
the incident. All the questions I had were about

feelings:
the feel of the gun, rocking in his hand. The feel of the
    blood, splashing
his face. The feel of his soul as it watched
another's leave, the feel of his
soul as it fell. These questions were not
rhetorical, not really. But still.

There was a shuffling behind us, as
we walked away. I didn't turn. Danny stopped,

glanced, but spotted nothing, &
kept on. We were going to be late for homeroom already, &
he couldn't afford to miss anything else.

Things had a way, you see, of piling up.

The world is collapsing around our ears . . .

We won! We won!
they cried, & I thought

I've heard this sound before.

    *   *   *

When asked for the scariest movie I've ever seen, I don't
    hesitate:
WarGames, 1983, featuring
a fresh-faced Matthew Broderick,
the always reliable Dabney Coleman, & a sexy
but not-yet-creepy-sexy Ally Sheedy.

    *   *   *

Avoiding the rising cheers, Rose & I pushed
our way through the crowded sidewalk, & snuck
around the side of Frank's Deli, into the narrow alley
to the parking lot. The dumpster was empty, which was a
    blessing.

The marching band was in fine form, & we
could just make out the tips of those little puffs on their
    hats as they
marched down the street. It wasn't much of a parade, but
    then,
it wasn't much of a town either.

    *   *   *

WarGames—young kid playing with computers sneaks into
government networks—most of us

didn't even know the word hacking in '83,
& the difference between a whiz kid's fingers caressing a
    keyboard
& a wizard wielding his wand seemed negligible.

Kid stumbles onto a program designed to remove human
    element
from control of nuclear weapons, & of course is minutes
    away
from provoking end of the world
before the machine
is miraculously taught
some games simply cannot be won.

Watched the movie, got a ride home, glanced up at the
    contrails
left by planes sweeping across the sky, mumbled
    something
to my mother on my way in, & finally
sat with my dad to watch Reagan sternly
warn Soviets against involvement in some nation or
    another,

then calmly proceeded to crawl underneath my bed,
where I determined to remain
indefinitely.

At that age I was just small enough
no one could really get a good hold on me,
& my teeth, though not yet full-sized,
had grown in fairly sharp. I announced repeatedly
I would not hesitate to use them.

*   *   *

Rose was a church person & once or twice a week extended
an invitation to a family picnic, a youth potluck, or
    something called
evening vespers, which I was never really clear on.
    Eventually I stopped
bothering with quickly invented excuses, as they fooled no
    one.

But as always, she never held it against me.

        *   *   *

My sister was finally able to coax me out from under the
    bed
with some calm words, a plateful of cookies,
& a large glass of ice cold 7UP.

        *   *   *

Mr. Johnson was obese, rooted to his seat,
spoke with the whistling whine of a condescending dog.
Gave no handouts, wrote nothing
on his dusty untouched blackboard—

even his pop quizzes required
hand-cramping long-form essays. No one could recall
seeing him outside his classroom, or even
out of his enormous groaning chair.

We all adored him.

        *   *   *

I wanted to be a believer. I wanted:
to care, to be seized by paralyzing grip

of faith, of certainty, of unfathomable love
for things unseen yet indisputably

known. But it always just left me
cold.

*   *   *

Mr. Johnson, you see, was the first adult who
would ask an opinion,
whether on the specific wording of the Magna Carta
or the energy legacy of Jimmy Carter,
& actually hear our answers, who gave us
the dignity of ferociously arguing to prove us wrong,
or dispensing an enthusiastic chuckle when we stumbled
into some minor semblance of truth. He might agree,
he might just call us a bunch of morons, but
without fail he heard us, which was more
than we dreamed
any teacher would bother to do.

School began to slip into summer,
even Honors History threatened to lose its appeal,
& there we sat, discussing the world everyone swore
was expanding all around us. Freedom, the newscasters
    sang,
was off her leash, racing
to cover the world in her bold, comforting light.
    Communism,
a horror in our minds only the slightest step down from
    Darth Vader-ism,
was on retreat, soon to fade
into the irrelevancy we were convinced it deserved.
In the streets of Beijing students shook the world,
(*students* shook the world!)

& Mr. Johnson & every one of my classmates assured
me as we scribbled in our notebooks
that this bad thing would fall apart,
that this corrupt center could not hold,
that mere capitalism would be loosed upon this, the best of
    all possible worlds.

*   *   *

There was a part of Rose drawn
to my struggle, such as it was. I don't mean to imply
she planned to go full missionary on me; that wouldn't
be fair to her. I think there was something
in the fervor of my hope & failure
that pulled at her, that forced her
to see through all the trappings & ornament of religion,
straight into the heart of her true faith.

She hoped, someday,
to meet me there.

*   *   *

Sitting in Mr. Johnson's class,
I felt so evil, so petty,
so fucking cynical. Because

I doubted. Because
I alone believed
that all we had studied
mattered,

that the arc of the amoral universe may be long but
it bends, unflinchingly,
toward terror.

They laughed at me. I still hear that sound,
so certain, so clear, so goddamn
American.

& then, of course, the end came, & laughter,
as is all too often the case, began to slide, almost
    imperceptibly, into tears.

*   *   *

Rose invited me to a service, the night
before the first desert bombs
fell. When I agreed to come, we were both too shocked
to make a big deal of it, & we settled into the pew,
her parents a few discreet rows ahead. The candles
    wavered, shook,
& the whole church seemed to sway, though
not to any music I could make out. & here,
a roomful of people—to be clear—a roomful of White people,
each one as filled with belief as Rose,
all sat together, held space in a way I
had only dreamt of, & cried
as they prayed for the safety
of people darker than me. & I

did not pray. Oh, I bowed my head. Repeated any words
I was told to, sang along from the hymn book,
even stood up front & read pages
they laid out for me. But as beautiful as it was, as forever
    as it felt,
I could not convince myself
it meant anything
beyond those walls of stained glass & bloodred brick,
or that whatever magic we found existed
beyond the pleading hearts
seated so safely inside.

*   *   *

U-S-A! U-S-A! U-S-A!

That, too, was familiar, by now.

We sat on the steps of the side entrance to the deli.
She put her head down
on my chest, & we watched everyone pass us by,

& it was there, under the sounds
of pep-rally America, that we shared
our first kiss.

The parade died & then the sun set & we
sat. & I

no longer cared if I believed, I only
held her as tight as I could, & was glad
that for now, we could both
let that be enough.

Subtle innuendos follow

Strange to allow myself to
sit & remember outgrown desire, to force

myself to lose
the smothering feel of

it, forget the ease of
forgetting, having that other

me to
blame, the burnt-out wreckage of

a life made solely from emotion,
no thought—because I have to think

so much more now.

Not deeper, just
more.

That last line of course
is why

being sober even now still shocks
the system. What I need most is to

see where this poem
ends—I want to

read finalized words I want to
know all the things I refused to

tell myself I want to
drown

in the miracle of
my own survival.

& so, by the way, I thank you

It wasn't much, just
that slight lift of eyebrows.

But friendships have been built on less,
& in the end it's that image alone
I hold onto.

     *   *****   *****

The metalheads preferred to set up outside the west wing
    bathrooms,
by the metalshop & the art studio, which made sense,
    really,
as they liked to debate the merits of their more gruesome
drawings & surprisingly light
paintings displayed behind glass
in a large case running down the hallway.

The bathrooms were not the biggest but still decent sized,
tucked away near the least-used back door, just far enough
from everything else to stay last on any time-concerned
    janitorial
schedule.

Besides, if a student was gonna smoke,
they did it in these restrooms, & no custodian
was gonna take responsibility for noticing that.

     *   *****   *****

If I dated someone for a few months, & it ended,
poorly or well, lazily or with hostile nonchalance,
with apathetic disregard or passionate unyielding hatred,

afterwards, people would stop by,
share a drink, give a hug, tell me

There are plenty of other fish in the sea

& other well-intended blandnesses, maybe even take me
   out
for a well-deserved night on the town.

When friendships end,
what are we left with?

What to do
when someone closer than blood
is gone,
fades away,

becomes something
distant?

Rose pulled me along. She was proud of her work
grinding & clipping thin sheets of metal into a blossoming
   feathery version of her namesake,
hanging now by the main entrance to the metalshop.
The instructor only selected one or two pieces a month,
a fierce competition she had consistently lost for years.
   Now, in that hallway,
her eyes saw only her work, while I
could never afford to not see everything.

What to do
when someone closer than blood

is gone, yet
still there?

* * *

A young woman with blond hair that burst
from shamelessly dark roots to waterfall over her eyes,
themselves a wonder of thick mascara sliding into
    vibrantly red lids,
caught Rose studying the sculpture & slid over
to discuss the finer points of plier techniques & soldering
    irons.

Two guys she was with glanced at each other, & nodded to
    a third,
leaning against the case behind me. My back yearned for
    the wall but Rose
held my hand in the firm obliviousness of one who has
    never before felt
under threat—or rather, who has never felt
under this specific threat.

The guys chuckled, continued
their loud talk about some band
I would most assuredly
never listen to, but their eyes were trained
on the Black guy with the White girl in front of them.
& then Pete

laughed
as he emerged from the bathroom, drying hands
on a rolled-up paper towel.

* * *

It wasn't much, just
that slight lift of eyebrows.

*   *   *

The young woman with the blond hair
bounced to Pete, & he pulled her in for a kiss.
Then,

a nod got a nod in return,
a quick glance at Rose then back to me.

I shrugged,
& we both
smiled, & returned

to our new lives.

When they reminisce over you

The phone was for me. This, obviously, made no sense; it never
was for me. Side-eye from my sister
said as much, & I stared
at the receiver as I took it from her. She didn't even have
to tell me her car was heading to school in minutes, whether
my ass was in a seat or not.

It was Danny, which made less sense.

Hey,
I said.

He said,
Meet me outside homeroom.

Danny never was one to say important shit over a phone.

                *   *   *

No one looked at me in the hallways. Streams of students
    parted
Red Sea-style, lines evaporated when I arrived, doors were
    held,

not a word spoken. It's funny
how something you dream of
can be a sign of horror when brought to actual life.

There is no police work like the quick gossip of a bored
    high school.

Everyone knew, in minutes. Before the papers or radio had
    anything,
we knew.

Which one do you think,
I asked Danny,
which one did it? Like,
pulled the trigger?

He looked at me, & didn't bother.
If anyone knew the answer, we did.

*   *   *

A 17-year-old girl & a 18-year-old man are sought in
connection with the execution-style killing yesterday of a
New York cabdriver, the police said.

The police said the couple got into the victim's cab in
Manhattan & drove 25 miles with him into Fanwood. The
cabdriver, H***** K****, 36, was shot about 10 P.M. on
an affluent street, said Capt. M. of the Fanwood Police
Department.

*   *   *

I found myself wandering by those bathrooms near the art
   room; I hadn't intended to.
A pair of metalheads roamed the hallway,
& I recognized
their shellshocked expressions from my face
in the mirror.

I nodded to the one I'd seen before & he staggered over.

Hey,
I said,
but then had to reach forward to snatch him as he sagged.
   I guided him
into a slump along the wall.

91

Figure you don't understand any more than me.

His broken eyes searched mine, as if they possessed
some hidden knowledge that would prove it all a bad joke,
   a hoax,
just another set-up by The Man to take down an innocent.

You & Pete close?

He nodded, then
shrank, reconsidered,

& stood, proud, to give
one more, firmer nod.

*　*　*

*"They shot him once in the head, execution-style," Captain M.
   said. "We're still investigating why."*

*　*　*

*Pete always called you,
& I had to lean in to hear,
his brother from another mother.*

Once upon a time,
I said.

What happened?

I smiled.

Life, I guess.

*　*　*

Details were spotty. The cab was found
dumped back in The City, driven there in an attempt
to throw cops off the scent.

Rumors, however, could never be shaken.

*   *   *

Math class was halfway over when I just walked out.

Ms. Wolfe stared, stuttered something
at my slowly disappearing back. She only knew me
sober,

an exemplary student, homework in early,
hand raised, the kind
she bragged about while finishing
her last cigarette in the cluttered teacher's lounge.

Danny was waiting for me outside the school.

*   *   *

The hard thing, of course, was the question. The important
    one
was not the how. Things

happened,
sometimes.

Ugly things, accidents & angers, & they couldn't
be taken back. We knew the fog
of life, of instant decisions
made under influence
of pain
& self-medication,

& all the regrets reality brings.

It wasn't even the why. Once you're that fucking high, in
    that car,
lacking money, you've set your course racing
along tracks your arms have borne far too long for you
to escape. In the end, there is no why.
The only real question, you see,

remains us.

*   *   *

I was—
said Danny,

I mean I am
but he couldn't finish but then he didn't need
to finish he only needed to cry on my shoulder so that's
    what he did.

*   *   *

I sat at the base of a tree, curled up in the woods
in front of my house.

Fireflies danced, a cricket called out to them, then a distant
    mother
loudly announced dinner to a distracted child.

Discussions, implications, inquiries, & interrogations
awaited as soon as I stepped through my own door.

They could wait.

Where did it switch? Where did I slip
free, sneak away? What hold did fate have on Pete that missed

me? Was there one moment, or ten? A single, solitary
    instant, or
simply a clean & inevitable ending?

He always called you
his brother from another mother.

& then
I could feel Pete's hand, softly touching

my shoulder once more, & it all fell on me,
a shattered lifetime's worth of rage & regret pouring

over me, burrowed in those cracks in my mind.
& how many times must I find myself

wishing I could remember
just when we stopped
being cute?

A white hot spotlight

Those flashing red-&-blues. Abandoned school
encircled, surrounded.

Stayed back, ducked
against a freshly planted tree, slipped

into dancing shadows. Couldn't
get close, but then

didn't need to.

*   *   *

The shame of actions taken
when you didn't know better

doesn't burn in the moment. No, it
simmers, crusts over, syrupy sweet,

the heavy load you bear until
that long-awaited explosion.

*   *   *

They led him out, hands
before him, sweatshirt

over the cuffs, that ridiculous act of preserving
tiny measures of dignity.

Pete's eyes shone through the dark.

*   *   *

On nights like these, when the air
lay dead against our skin, & we

could not see the night sky for the strobing lights, our future
appeared solid, defined, immovable, we could no longer dream

that anything mattered.

    *   *   *

A clink as I bumped the trunk of an older, thicker
    tree—reached
& grabbed the bottle from back pocket. Tore the wrapping,
cracked the cap, twisted open.

For you, Pete.

Poured a shot, two, three
onto the bark, turned & hurled the bottle

to die in an unseen side street.

    *   *   *

Alright, you motherfuckers,
he said,
who's next?

    *   *   *

A few cops jumped, flashlights
whipping around to scan the distance. In their glow,

receiving thanks, pats on the back,
way-to-go-man,
was Jimmy Peterson.

Pretty sure he was laughing, but sometimes
that can be hard to tell from tears,
if we're being honest.

* * *

It is a difficult thing,
with today's eyes, to see

the way we used to view
ourselves.

* * *

Nothing left. Hands in pockets.
Turn.

& walk
home.

You, you said you'd wait until the end of the world

Sorry I didn't come sooner.

He waved that off.

I laid out what I had been able to get from the vending
     machines—
     chips, candy bars, a packet of fruit & nuts, a couple
     Cokes,
     & one very big & crumbly chocolate chip cookie.

He popped open a Coke, took a gulp, then another, bigger one.
Tore into a Butterfinger.

I stared at the cookie. It was already falling apart inside its
     plastic wrap. How old was it? This was not the best
     choice I
     could have made.

     It did have chocolate chips, though. That had to count
     for something.

I looked around, at all the men in the room, & thought
     of the deals they'd been forced to make. Guys in
     orange uniforms, guys in blue-black uniforms with
     weapons to match, guys in their best clothes,
     like me.

We had good times,
he said.

We did,
I said. *We did indeed.*

He leaned forward, but looked
to the windows. They were large &
institutional, covered
with wire mesh, & the day outside was blue, though
the morning sun couldn't be seen from the angle
the windows faced.

Every so often a random bird flitted
past & everyone's eyes locked

onto it, following from window to
window, until

it flew away
into the sky.

We still play our little games

America you've given me all & now
I'm nothing.

America I used to be your bastard I'm
not sorry.

    *   *   *

Outside biology I finally caught up with Jimmy Peterson,
some idiot nudged his shoulder, & we
stared each other down.

This is for Pete.
Snitches, stitches,
I said,
you know the deal.

Then all around us so much
silence. I felt myself smile
as I walked away.

    *   *   *

America when will you be
angelic?

Pete is in East Jersey State now I don't think
he'll come back it's sinister.

America when will we be worthy
of Standing Rock?

    *   *   *

I find myself remembering Dude.

A little over a year before it all ended,
lunchtime.

We kept a few steps back from Dude, but
no one got between us in the cafeteria line. Pete
made the first crack,

probably about Dude's dangling
earrings—we all had the left pierced 'cuz that
was cool, but he had both, which

you just didn't do. Dude had on
a scarf, which was just about
the end for me, & his
nails were prettier than both girls he went
everywhere with.

America are you being sinister or
is this some form of practical joke?
I've given up trying
to get to the point.

America free Leonard Peltier.

I said

Dude wears that blouse better than my sister does

& it was all over for Jimmy Peterson
who laughed too hard to do too much else. Danny
just watched Pete. But Dude said nothing,

so we assumed they couldn't hear until
the taller of the two girls turned on us
& said

Enough!

America this is the impression I get from
looking at The Huffington Post.

America this is quite serious. It occurs to me that
I too am America.

I am yelling at myself again.

But then Dude
calmly took the taller of the two girls by the arm & led
her toward the salads.

Don't even bother.

The cute one whined—
Anthony—
& he took her arm as well.

I know who I am,
he said,
& I like it. They're still too dumb to know they don't.

America why are your librarians
full of tears?

America how can I write my screaming
poem in your boring mood?

*   *   *

I know who I am,
he said.

They're still too dumb
to know they don't.

*   *   *

In the end, Jimmy Peterson
ran. That was unexpected.

A shove against a locker, & Jimmy Peterson
was gone. But he had never been
fast, I stayed on him as we raced down
hallways & hallways & eventually
he found himself stuck
behind a surprisingly tiny girl playing
a tuba strapped to her waist &
a very large fellow jamming along on a piccolo.

*   *   *

America my mind is made up there's going to be trouble.
You should have seen me reading Fanon.

America I feel sentimental about Occupy.

*   *   *

Jimmy Peterson
covered up, I got a few shots in, &

he took off, this time
as soon as he made it round the corner he threw open a
    door &
dove in. I skittered to a stop in
the doorway, Jimmy Peterson
clambered
to the back of the room, &

three teachers looked up
from coffee mugs in shock &
I turned back & straight

into a screaming hollering crowd

Fight! Fight! Fight!

* * *

America stop pushing I know
what I am.

* * *

I hadn't seen the crowd form, though I
had been a part of so many I
should have known. I

had not yet been on this side before,
& the greedy straining horror of it all was complicated
by the crowd's happiness, pleasure,
their immediate shrieking
satisfaction.

* * *

America you don't really want
to go to war.

*   *   *

There was a mirror in the back of the room,
but I couldn't bear to let it
look at me.

*   *   *

America everyone's too serious even me. But now I
can't stand my own mind &
it just makes me sick of your insane
demands.

*   *   *

The crowd was so joyous, so gleeful,
so expectant,

so hyped,

it didn't even recognize me when I
snuck through,
crept my way to the back, even

lifted my voice
once or twice to
blend in—
not one of them could tell

the fighting was already over.

*   *   *

America after all it is you
& I who are perfect not
the next world,

even if we're both still too dumb to know it.

106

EPILOGUE

I THOUGHT WE'D GET TO SEE FOREVER . . .

Close your eyes, give me your hand, darling.
Do you feel my heart beating? Do you understand?

—The Bangles,
"Eternal Flame"

Excuse me for a moment, I'm in another world

There is only so much night and so she promises to
save the last dance for the Zebra and

somehow she is here and
I can't really explain how I got here too and

I want to stay, to stay in her life always and
then she whispers *Yellow*

is the color of sunrays and
I sing along and

she doesn't care that I can't really sing along and
for some reason she actually likes the way I dance and

the DJ says he'll play all night but
there's never been enough night and

when her dress tears she takes off my tie and
makes something new and

never misses a beat and
I still can't believe she said yes and

we are a we and
everyone's watching and

I think I may just have
to kiss her all night but

then I remember there's never enough night so
we'll have to find a way to make it last and

she promises to save that dance for the Zebra and
I can't imagine asking for more and

her breath is on my ear and
her body is on mine and

it's our time, time today and

I whisper please let there be enough night, just this night,
please let it be that night, that one night,

that endless long night, that never here tomorrow,
that last night, that best night, tonight.

I don't need you to worry for me 'cuz I'm alright

I have never been comfortable
being honest. This

has been awkward,
as it is listed first

in the job description for poet.

I've never been comfortable
being a poet either, but that's okay,

as being uncomfortable with poetry is,
surprisingly, listed second

in the poet's job description.

Simpler to be
truthful than honest, though

the line is deliberately blurred. There
are worlds &

loves & whole lives left out, &

that has to be okay, or
nothing gets finished. Things have

changed, I've gotten
old,

& that has been
wonderful.

In the end,
growing up,

like manhood,
was never a given—but then

neither
was it an option.

After: all

I wrote the forgiveness I have been unable to
live, for myself most of all. Feelings remain unclear—

the reason I must rely on words to speak my truth. But now,
real truth: poems, like wars, never end. They lie

in wait, hidden within bruised hearts & lost
personal histories until sparked awake by

unforeseen relapse of pain & forgetfulness. We
modeled who we were on what we saw &

back then, we didn't know anyone who
remembered. Now, memory is all we

have been left with—& it has never been trustworthy. But
this story, like all stories, is simply a memory straightened
    out,

beaten on the anvil of what should have been, until
we are left with something we can wrap up neatly & say,

This here is my story—take it, & thank you
for caring.

NOTES

With gratitude, I acknowledge the following inspiring samples and sources:

"The Youth Are Getting Restless" by Bad Brains
"Don't Believe the Hype" by Public Enemy
"Friends" by Whodini
"Invincible" by Pat Benatar
"Straight to Hell" by The Clash
"Colors" by Ice-T
"Sign Your Name" by Terence Trent D'Arby
"White Lines (Don't Don't Do It)" by Melle Mel
"Total Eclipse of the Heart" by Bonnie Tyler
"Hand to Mouth" by George Michael
"99 Red Balloons" by Nena
"Hey Young World" by Slick Rick
"Born to Run" by Bruce Springsteen
"Mad World" by Tears for Fears
"Glory Days" by Bruce Springsteen
"Born in the U.S.A." by Bruce Springsteen
"We Are the Champions" by Queen
"Prophets of Rage" by Public Enemy
"Ice Cream Castles" by The Time
"6 in the Mornin'" by Ice-T
"Barbarism Begins at Home" by The Smiths
"1999" by Prince
"Fly on the Windscreen" by Depeche Mode
"Radio Song" by REM & KRS-One

"Goody Two Shoes" by Adam Ant

"That's What Friends Are For" by Dionne Warwick

"They Reminisce over You (T.R.O.Y.)" by Pete Rock & C.L.
Smooth

"Big Shot" by Billy Joel

"I Am the Owl" by Dead Kennedys

"Until the End of the World" by U2

"It's So Hard to Say Goodbye to Yesterday" by Boyz II Men

"Eternal Flame" by The Bangles

"Don't Disturb This Groove" by The System

"Keep On Movin'" by Soul II Soul

"My Life" by Billy Joel

ACKNOWLEDGMENTS

First, I have to thank my loving and lovely wife, Christy Santoro, for being by my side, for being in my life, for always saving that last dance for me.

Zel and Elio—your beauty, fierceness, and unwavering belief in art meant everything to me. Becoming your father made me a better person and a better writer.

Thanks to DuiJi Mshinde and Jeni McFarland for their kind words on the cover and constant support, and much love to my homie Nico Amador for his stunning and moving foreword to this book. The fact that artists such as yourselves would speak for my work means more than I could ever express—my endless gratitude to you all.

Thanks and acknowledgment to the editors and staff of the following publications where these poems first appeared:

"A self-made monster" appeared in *The Northern Virginia Review*, Spring 2018 Vol. 32.

Much love to *Philadelphia Stories* for publishing "Past the days of yes y'allin' (Jersey Verse Part Three)" in Winter 2018, and "Peace is a dream (Kids in America Part One)" in Winter 2019: 27, and for their overall support for myself and all Philly writers.

"There ain't no need for ya" was published by *8-West Press* in Spring 2018.

"We can't afford to be innocent" was featured in the inaugural *Cultureshare* by The Free Library of Philadelphia in November 2017.

I must thank the people of CavanKerry Press for believing in this book, and for all of the time and energy the entire press has put into this work. When I wrote this book, it was as a lone artist struggling with expressing my thoughts and concerns in a way that mattered. Having their support, new ideas, and skills has made this a book I could never have done on my own. Gabe Cleveland has been a constant presence, from the first phone call to tell me the book was accepted all the way to publication. Baron Wormser made vital suggestions in editing both poems and the manuscript as a whole—those contributions were crucial. Joy Arbor did the legwork in copyediting, which I know I needed. Extra thanks to Ryan Scheife for the brilliant cover.

Shout out to Simone Zelitch, who taught me how to write and how to teach writing, and the rest of the faculty at Community College of Philadelphia. A shout-out as well to Rutgers-Camden's MFA program, for continually pushing and encouraging me. Muriel Shockley and so many others at Goddard College helped me keep my head on straight as I tried to figure out just who I am.

CAVANKERRY'S MISSION

A not-for-profit literary press serving art and community, CavanKerry is committed to expanding the reach of poetry and other fine literature to a general readership by publishing works that explore the emotional and psychological landscapes of everyday life, and to bringing that art to the underserved where they live, work, and receive services.

OTHER BOOKS IN THE EMERGING VOICES SERIES

This book was printed on paper from responsible sources.